STAGE
6
BOOK 2

NO WAY TO WEIGH A WHALE

John Townsend

228246 EN
No Way To Weigh A Whale

Townsend, J

ATOS BL: 2.8
Points: 0.5   MY

RISING ⭐ STARS

"Listen up!" Oz shouted as he came through the door. He threw his arms up and clapped. "I've got good news. We've got a job at The Barge Inn."

There were yelps and cheers all around the room. "So what's the catch, Oz?" Asad called.

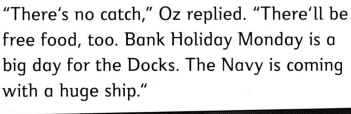

"There's no catch," Oz replied. "There'll be free food, too. Bank Holiday Monday is a big day for the Docks. The Navy is coming with a huge ship."

"Dockside Day will bring crowds and lots of events," Oz went on. "We've been asked to run Club OK Night at The Barge Inn. So who's up for it?" There were more yelps and cheers.

Miss Evans added, "We thought some of you might do a show. We've asked Beth's dad to be DJ and Taz wants to get a band together. Some of you could sing, dance, tell jokes."

Anna called, "I don't think you ought to tell Jack. Here he comes now."

Jack ran into the room. "Hey, hear this ... my gran nearly drowned just now when she was making a fruit cake. She fell in the mixing bowl and was dragged right under by a very strong **currant**."

Maya stared at him. "I never get your jokes, Jack," she frowned.

"It's a pun," Jack laughed. "That means mixing up two words that sound the same. Like **currant** — a raisin thing — and a **current** that you get in a river."

"I still don't think it's funny," she said.

Jack tried again. "Did you hear about the whale that went to Weight Watchers? In just a week it ate eight tons of food and had grown so huge, no scales were big enough to weigh it. So it got on a train and went all the way to the 'whale weigh station'. Get it? **Railway — whale weigh!** It took ages to find how heavy it was — it was such a **wait. Weight!** Get it? It was so upset it began to **wail. Whale!** Get it?"

They all gave a groan. Maya shook her head. "You're just not funny, though. Your jokes are really weak today," she sighed.

"Jack's jokes are always rough," Caleb grinned. "They're so old!"

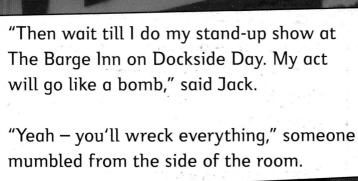

"Then wait till I do my stand-up show at The Barge Inn on Dockside Day. My act will go like a bomb," said Jack.

"Yeah — you'll wreck everything," someone mumbled from the side of the room.

"I've thought of a cool name for my band," Taz called out. "How about 'The Banned'? That's a pun, too. Do you get it?" Taz tried to explain, "Not **band** but **banned** – like **not allowed**. Get it?"

"**Not aloud**?" Maya said. "So no one will hear you? That's thoroughly mad!"

"Do you know what, Taz?" Jack said, tapping his nose. "I'll let you into a secret. You and me are wasted here. It's tough when no one knows just how great we are. We'll be stars one day and reach the height of fame. I know both of us are about to hit The Barge Inn like a bomb. You just see!"

Bank Holiday Weekend

It was the day before the big event. Brad, Taz and Jack were setting up the stage at The Barge Inn. They'd brought a drum kit, sound desk and lights. Jack had even bought paints to make posters.

CLUB OK PRESENTS

Dockside FUN Night
at The Barge Inn

NO WAY TO WEIGH A WHALE!
(AND OTHER GREAT JOKES)
STARRING JACK BILTON (STAND-UP COMIC)

BETH HILL (SINGER)
&

TAZ HILL'S THE BANNED

Just as Jack stood on stage to run through his jokes, Nadia ran in. "Brad," she whispered, "we need to empty the building. They've dredged the docks and dragged up a bomb from World War 2. The Army is about to blow it up on the marshes."

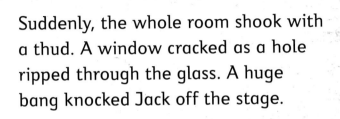

Suddenly, the whole room shook with a thud. A window cracked as a hole ripped through the glass. A huge bang knocked Jack off the stage.

"Wow!" Taz cried. "You were right, Jack. Your old jokes are a real blast from the past!"

CHECK

1. What was Oz's good news?

2. What was Jack's joke about his gran?

3. Where do you weigh a whale according to Jack's joke?

4. What did Taz want to call his band?

5. Where was the show going to be held?

6. Why did Nadia run into the room?

7. Why did Jack's joke go with a bang?

FIND

Find the **verbs** to fill the gaps.

1. He _____ his arms up and clapped. (page 2)

2. They'd _____ a drum kit, sound desk and lights. (page 18)

3. Jack had even _____ paints. (page 18)

What's missing?

1. so whats the catch oz asad called   (page 3)

2. i still dont think its funny she said   (page 9)

3. do you know what taz jack said
tapping his nose   (page 16)

*Find the **nouns** to fill the gaps.*

1. There were more yelps and _____ .   (page 5)

2. No _____ were big enough to weigh it.
(page 10)

3. Your _____ are really weak today.   (page 12)

4. The Army is about to blow it up on the _____ .
(page 19)

Which word in the story means

1. lots of people?　(page 5)

2. moan or weep?　(page 10)

3. destroy or ruin?　(page 13)

4. shuddered?　(page 21)

*Swap the word in **bold** for a new word that means the opposite.*

5. "I still don't think it's **funny**," she said.

6. Your jokes are really **weak** today.

7. "Brad," she **whispered**.

8. A real **blast** from the past.